TOADS TEACH THE TANGO

KATIE RUTLEDGE OVERGARD

ISBN: 978-0-692-96288-6

DEDICATION

This book is dedicated to the letter A, without U

I never could have completed any words.

M and N were a bit of a pain,

but once we hashed out their contracts they settled down.

Z was an absolute joy to work with and L is going to need to apologize before starring

in another one of my books. Seriously.

Also, this is for my kids, Addison and William.

Without them, I never would have needed to teach anyone their letters.

TOADS TEACH THE TANGO

A BOOK OF LAUGHABLE LETTER PLAY

Alligators appreciate abstract art.

Bears bake the best blueberry banana bread.

Camels crave caramel cake.

Dogs delight in disco dancing.

Elephants eagerly eat eggs, every kind.

Foxes feel fashionable in fedoras.

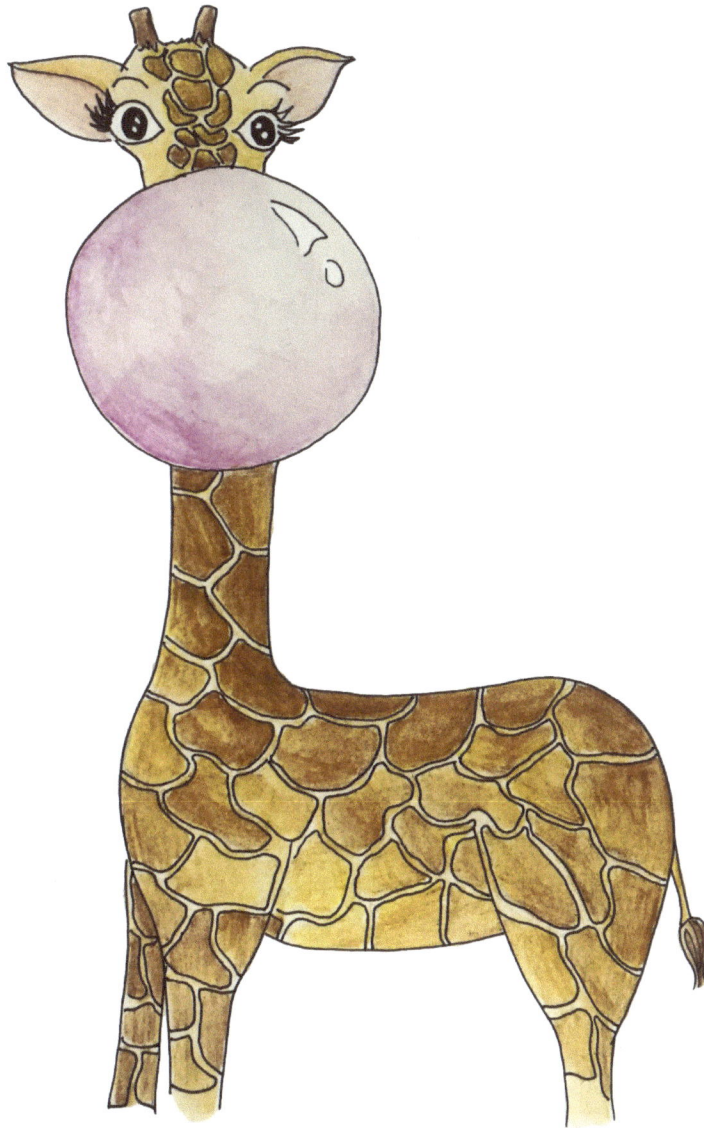

Giraffes get goofy with grape gum.

Hedgehogs hide their huge hoards of hardcover books.

Iguanas imagine indigo ice cream.

Jellyfish juggle juicy jellybeans.

Kangaroos enjoy kiwis covered in ketchup.

Llamas love lounging with lattes.

Mice make moist mini mango muffins.

Narwhals nibble nectarines while reading nordic novels.

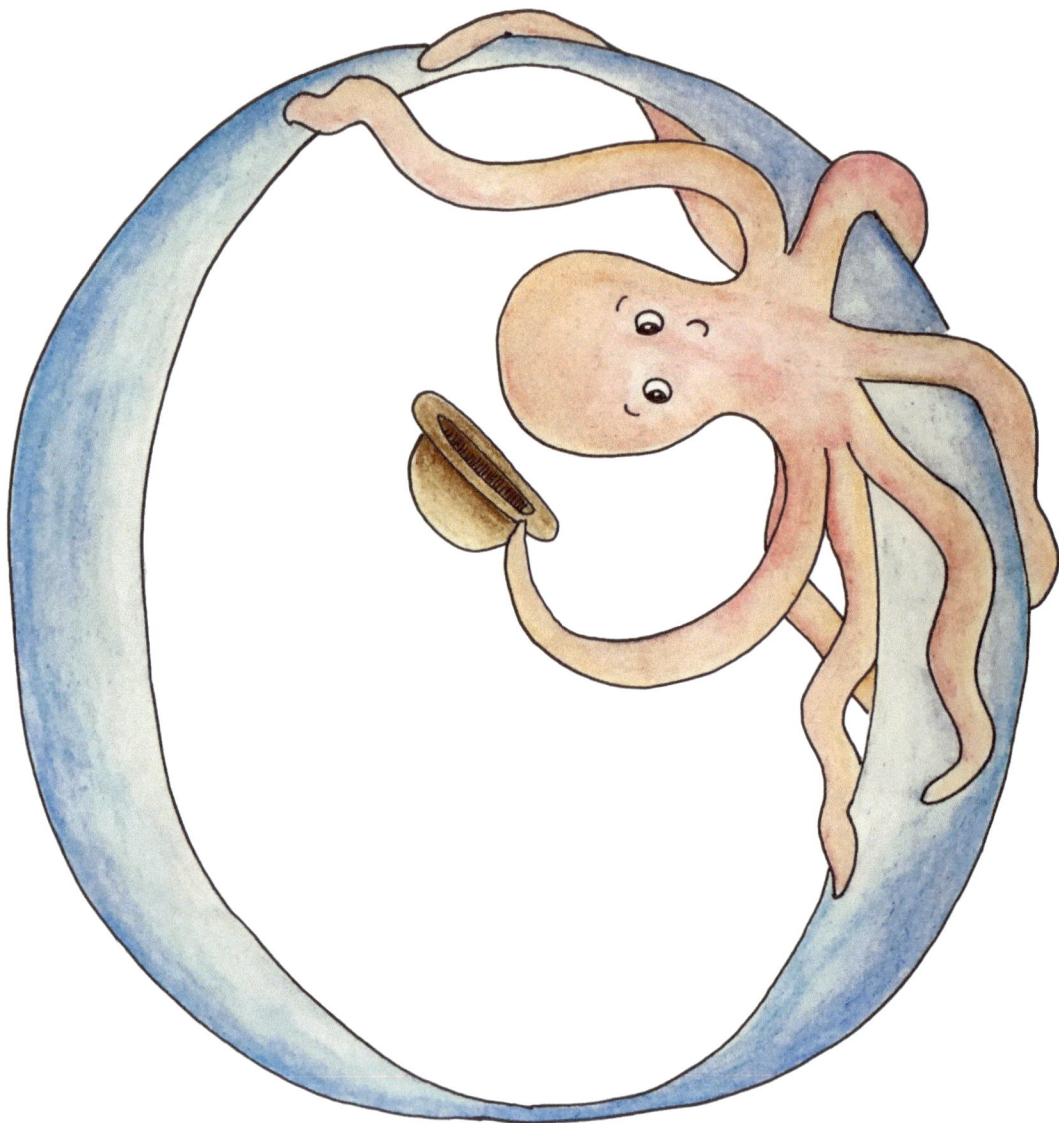

Octopuses are offended by odd odors.

Pigs prefer painting purple pears.

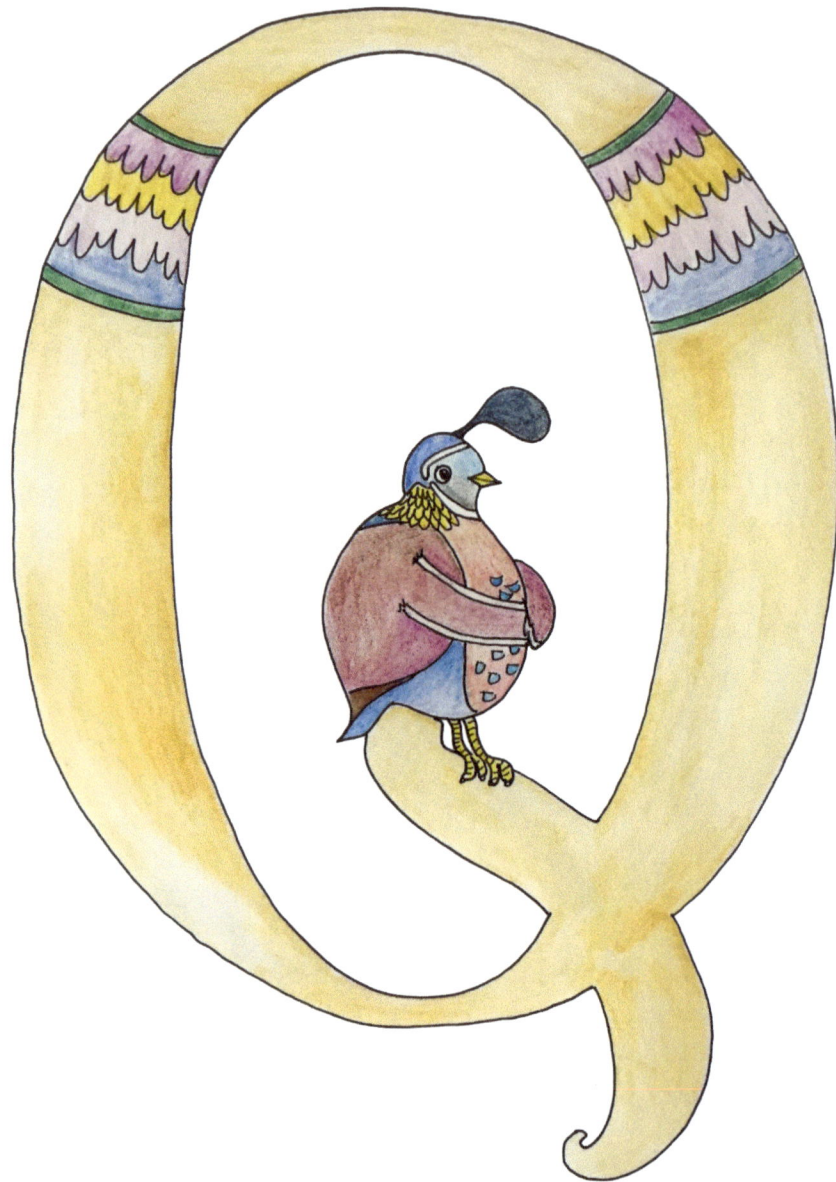

Quails quilt quickly, with quite a lot of quality.

Raccoons regularly relax in red raincoats.

Squirrels are most satisfied in soft sweaters, sipping strawberry tea.

Turtles take their time when typing, typically.

Unicorns usually wear uniforms on their unicycles.

Vultures play the violin while wearing violet vests.

Walruses wear whimsical wizard hats while waving their wands.

Xantus hummingbirds play the xylophone,

they're experts.

X words are hard.

Yaks yearn to feel youthful in yellow.

Zebras zig zag through the zinnias.

ABOUT THE AUTHOR

Katie likes to laugh. She thinks that things are always better when they're a little silly. She and her husband, Chris, want to make sure that their kids grow up with a good sense of humor and healthy understanding of sarcasm. They have already succeeded, those kids can zip a zinger at you with the best of 'em.

Katie also loves reading. And beautiful handwriting and stories that transport the reader to far off places and presents ideas the reader has never thought of before. She spent a lot of time and brainpower in college learning about the importance of telling a story *really well* (at least she hopes so) and her parents are super thrilled that she is using her degree they paid for to write books. They think it's super cool.

Katie, Chris and their sarcastic kids live in Lone Tree, Colorado.

They read with their kids every night.

ACKNOWLEDGEMENTS

This book is dedicated to all the animals with names that start with a letter.
Without them, I never could have written a funny book about animals and the alphabet.

To my mom and dad, because they made me.

To Thayer, because she said I should draw animals and letters. Together.

To Diane, because she said I should make those drawings into a book.

To Chris, because I married him and I love him.

And my kids, Addison & William. Their names start with letters too.
They're pretty great.

(AND THANKS TO WILLIAM FOR THIS AWESOME ARTWORK)

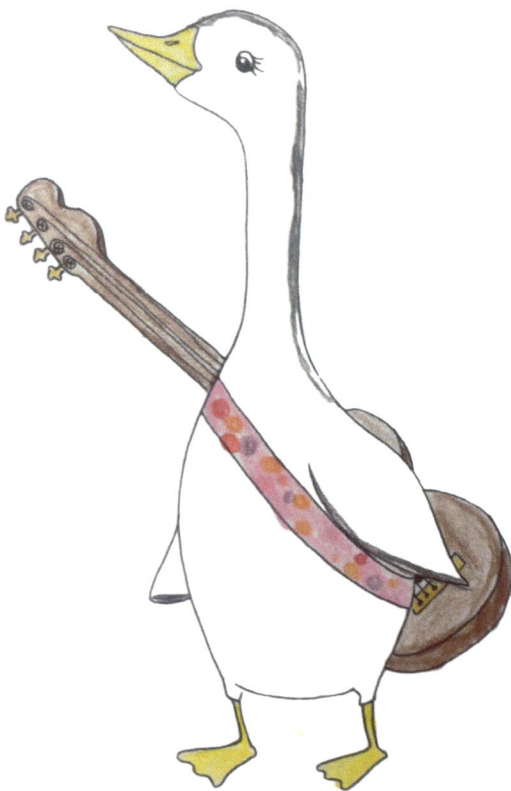

(ARTWORK COURTESY OF ADDIE "GOOSEY" OVERGARD)

I LOVE LETTERS.

Letters make words.

Words make books.

Books lead to ideas. And imagination and creativity and dreams of being someone who can change the world.

Sometimes we get caught up in everything we have to do as adults. We *must* pay the bills, its important that we wash our clothes and put gas in the car and make sure our kids wear clean underwear everyday. We have to empty the dishwasher and eat food numerous times a day. We have to work (sometimes doing something we care nothing about) and sit in traffic and listen to people talk who don't get the cues that its time to get off the phone.

We have to sit with our little ones and help them learn simple things like *letters* over and over and over.

And over again.

But we want them to love letters. We want them to know that learning is fun and exciting and that they can take these things they learn and do even MORE things with their new ideas.

We want them to sit with us and feel like Mom or Dad or Grandma or Great Uncle Joe adores sitting with them reading books. That they love it so much that they don't want to be anywhere else but *right here,* listening to a sweet little voice giggle at silly drawings and sentences while a thirsty little mind learns the sounds and shapes of the alphabet.

Read with your babies. Savor the way their hair smells as they lean against your chest. Feel their little hands - someday their hands will be as big as yours and not so easy to hold.

Show them that you love letters, and that you love reading with them.

Be there. In the moment. Don't miss it.

And never forget that toads are excellent dancers.

www.ingramcontent.com/pod-product-compliance
Lightning Source LLC
LaVergne TN
LVHW072111070426
835509LV00003B/116